TIME FOR KIDS

UNSOLVED!

Mysterious Places

Lisa Greathouse
Stephanie Kuligowski

Consultants

Timothy Rasinski, Ph.D.
Kent State University

Lori Oczkus
Literacy Consultant

Based on writing from *TIME For Kids. TIME For Kids* and the *TIME For Kids* logo are registered trademarks of TIME Inc. Used under license.

Publishing Credits

Dona Herweck Rice, *Editor-in-Chief*
Lee Aucoin, *Creative Director*
Jamey Acosta, *Senior Editor*
Heidi Fiedler, *Editor*
Lexa Hoang, *Designer*
Stephanie Reid, *Photo Editor*
Rane Anderson, *Contributing Author*
Rachelle Cracchiolo, *M.S.Ed., Publisher*

Image Credits: p.8 Corbis; pp.24–25 Dreamstime; p.10 Getty Images/Dorling Kindersley, p.15 (top) Reuters/Newscom; pp.17, 20, 36 Getty Images; pp.4 (bottom), 18, 22–23, 26 iStockphoto; p.16 Danita Delimont/Newscom; p.13 (bottom) AFP/Getty Images/Newscom; pp.28–29 akg-images/Newscom; p.21 Newscom; p.12 (bottom) SIP/SIPA/Newscom; p.12 (top) ZUMA Press/Newscom; p.13 (top) Photo Researchers Inc.; p.35 (top) The Granger Collection; All other images from Shutterstock.

Teacher Created Materials
5301 Oceanus Drive
Huntington Beach, CA 92649-1030
http://www.tcmpub.com

ISBN 978-1-4333-4828-0

Printed by: 51497
Printed in: China

Table of Contents

Mysteries You Can Visit

Lost **civilizations**. Missing airplanes. Buried pirate treasure. These sound like great mystery stories. But they are not fiction. They are reality. They exist in some of the world's most mysterious places.

In this book, you will trek through the mountains. You will search for a city below the sea. And you will look for signs of life on other planets. You are about to discover the secrets behind some of Earth's unexplained places.

Chaco Canyon

Angkor Wat

THINK LINK

Today we know a lot about the world, but there is also a lot we are still learning.

- How did people in the ancient world build monuments without modern tools?
- Have aliens visited Earth?
- What happened to lost cities like Angkor Wat, Atlantis, and Chaco?

Mysterious Monuments

People have always wanted to create things. They made fire, built crude tools, and wrote on cave walls. Then people began to think bigger. They made **monuments**. Statues are monuments made to honor someone. Early monuments paid respect to gods or rulers. Other statues were built to honor the dead.

New **technology** helped people build great stone structures. And now, these amazing places are proof of **ancient** human creativity.

Technology Through the Ages

Technology is anything that humans use to solve problems or make work easier. People first used technology when they turned sticks and stones into simple tools. Making fire was an advance in technology. So was the invention of the wheel. These were major technological discoveries in **prehistoric** times.

Sacred Stones

A circle of huge stones rises from the plains of England. This ancient monument is called Stonehenge. It has puzzled people for centuries.

Scientists know it was built 5,000 years ago. But everything else is a mystery. How did the builders move the huge stones? Some weigh more than 25 tons. And they came from 150 miles away! How did they stack them? And why did they work so hard to build this monument?

Some people think Stonehenge was a calendar. Many points match up with **astrological** events. Others say this was a burial place. **Archaeologists** have found human bones at the site.

Stonehenge as viewed from above

Other Ideas

The most accepted theory today is that Stonehenge was a burial site for ancient leaders. A more far-fetched theory suggests Merlin, the magician from the King Arthur legend, used magic to move the stones. Others say that aliens placed the stones.

Ancient Calendar

In 1965, an astronomer named Gerald Hawkins wrote a book called *Stonehenge Decoded*. In it, he linked 165 points at the site to astrological events. For example, at dawn on the summer **solstice**, the center ring, two nearby stones, and the sun all line up.

Where Kings Rest

Between 3,000 BC and 300 BC, Egypt was a vibrant place. Thousands of people lived along the Nile River. Their culture was rich and full of mysteries.

Today, millions of people visit Egypt every year. Many go to see the Great Pyramid of Giza. It was built 4,500 years ago. It was a royal **tomb** for Pharaoh Khufu. Several smaller pyramids lie around it.

But how was the pyramid built? It is 40 stories high. And it is made from more than 2 million stones. The biggest stones weigh as much as 2.5 tons. But they didn't have modern machines. So how did the ancient Egyptians build the pyramids?

A Big Job

It is believed that between 20,000 and 30,000 workers built the pyramids. The work took 20 years. The workers lived in villages nearby. The villages had bakers, butchers, brewers, and doctors.

The Way to Heaven

Egyptians built pyramids to keep their pharaohs' bodies, spirits, and riches safe. Ancient texts described pharaohs going to the afterlife. The pyramid shape is said to symbolize the rays of sunshine.

Egyptian Extras

The desert is a dry place with little moisture to wear down rocks. That is one reason the stone pyramids are so well preserved. The pyramids aren't the only mysteries from ancient Egypt. Researchers are still studying the land to learn more about these fascinating people.

the mask of King Tut

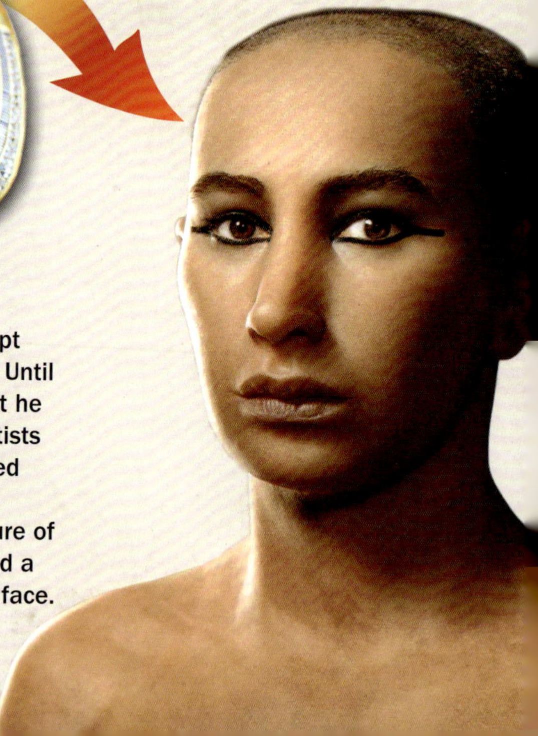

King Tutankhamen

A Pharaoh's Face

King Tutankhamen ruled Egypt more than 4,000 years ago. Until May 2005, no one knew what he looked like. A team of scientists scanned King Tut's mummified body. The readings gave information about the structure of his face. A sculptor then used a model to re-create King Tut's face.

Unlocking Language

The Rosetta Stone is an ancient rock that is nearly 2,000 years old. Egyptian law is carved into it in three languages. Before finding the Rosetta Stone, historians did not know how to translate Egyptian **hieroglyphics**. Finally, they were able to find patterns in the languages. The Rosetta Stone unlocked the key to reading hieroglyphics.

Eye in the Sky

Pictures taken from space helped an archaeologist search the deserts of Egypt. Over 15 pyramids were found buried under the sand. Powerful cameras detected different types of buried material.

Satellites capture images of Egypt from above. Infrared images reveal the buried layers of the ancient city Tanis.

Stone Guards

Easter Island lies in the South Pacific. It is thousands of miles from any other dry land. The first explorer in 1722 was shocked when he arrived. Hundreds of giant stone faces were staring at him from the shore.

The island holds 900 statues. They are known as **moai** (MOH-eye). The average moai is 13 feet tall and weighs about 13 tons. Some historians say the statues were built to honor the **chieftains** who once lived there. Others say they were **religious** symbols. Who built the statues? Why did they place them so they stare at the sea?

The Great Parent

Island lore says that the first residents came from Polynesia 1,500 years ago. A chief named Hotu Matu'a, which means "Great Parent," sailed thousands of miles in a double canoe. His wife and other family members came with him.

A Special Site

Easter Island is a world heritage site. It is on the United Nations Educational, Scientific and Cultural Organization (UNESCO) list. Hundreds of cultural and natural sites around the world are on the UNESCO list. Countries work together to protect these unique places.

Round Riddles

In the 1930s, nearly 300 stone spheres were found on a small island in Costa Rica. Some were as small as a marble. Others were as big as a car. But they are all almost perfectly round. The spheres seem carefully placed on the island. Small ones sit next to larger ones. Some spheres are alone.

There are many myths about the spheres. Locals believe a special potion was used to carve them. Maybe it helped to soften the rock. Others think the spheres came from the lost city of Atlantis. And some people say the perfect stone spheres were made by nature.

Alien Artifact?

The Klerksdorp Spheres are located in a mine in South Africa. Some are round in shape while others are like a disc. They are dated at three billion years old. That is long before humans existed on Earth! However, some people believe these stones could not have been made by nature. If they were made before humans walked the Earth, who could have made them?

Researchers believe the Costa Rican stone spheres are nearly 1,500 years old.

Disappearing Acts

A missing person is one thing. But lost cities are another. Some of the world's spookiest places have one thing in common—odd disappearances!

The Lost City

Machu Picchu (MAH-choo PEE-choo) sits in the misty mountains of Peru. This is the lost city of the Incas. It was forgotten for centuries. In 1922, explorers reached the city's palaces. They found temples. Inside one temple was the royal tomb. Explorers found pottery and the **remains** of gardens and homes, too. The city's walls, terraces, and ramps seem to have been carved into the mountain.

Machu Picchu was built by the Incan people around 1450. Then they left it 100 years later. Today, Machu Picchu is the top spot for tourists. But why was the city built? And why did the people leave?

Strange Sickness

Machu Picchu was **abandoned** shortly after the Spanish arrived in Peru. The Spanish never found the city in the mountains. But some experts believe they may have caused the city's downfall. It's possible the residents died from smallpox, a disease the Spanish introduced to the region.

Left Behind

A city once thrived in Chaco Canyon, New Mexico. This was long before Europeans arrived in America. People from around the area met up in Chaco. It was a busy city. People came there to trade and worship.

The Great Houses of Chaco may have been America's first public buildings. These were huge and many stories tall. They had hundreds of large rooms. It took workers decades to build them. Roads connected the city center to more than 150 houses.

Today, only ruins remain. What made the people leave the city they had worked so hard to build?

Sacred Spaces

The Great Houses of Chaco had many **kivas**. A kiva is a circular room used for religious ceremonies.

Climate Change

Climate change may have forced residents to leave Chaco. A long **drought** began in 1130 and lasted 50 years. The lack of rain would have made it impossible to grow enough food to feed many people.

city ruins in Chaco Canyon, New Mexico

Lost Land

Vanuatu is a small island in the South Pacific. Recently, an entire village had to relocate. Climate change made the sea rise. It flooded their homes. They had to move to a different part of the island.

City Beneath the Sea

Imagine a perfect island. The residents are great **architects**. Their palaces are works of art. So are their temples and bridges. Five rings of water lie around the island.

A philosopher named Plato wrote about such a place 2,500 years ago. It was called *Atlantis.* Without warning, Atlantis was gone. Many believe it sank into the sea. It happened "in a single day and a night," Plato wrote. Since then, people have been searching. They want to find the lost city of Atlantis. Many people have believed they found it. But they were wrong.

Was Atlantis a real place? Or, was it just a legend? And if it was real, where is the lost city today?

A Utopian City

Atlantis has captured many imaginations. Some scholars believe it was a **utopia**. Plato described it as a land rich in metals and other resources. It was surrounded by wealth and natural beauty. No wonder so many people are looking for it!

Island Mystique

According to ancient lore, Atlantis was an island with a strong military. Its technology and architecture were said to be very advanced. These qualities made it noteworthy. But its sudden disappearance beneath the sea made it **legendary**.

Some people imagine Atlantis might look like this if they found it today.

sculpture of Plato

Lost and Found

The legend of Atlantis has inspired books, movies, and investigations around the world. Recently, researchers traveled to Spain to learn more. Could this be the year the lost island is discovered?

Some researchers believe the ruins of Atlantis may be hidden under the mud flats of southern Spain, near the city of Cadiz.

Geologists used satellite and radar to map the area. Shadows under the mud suggest a ringed city may have once thrived there.

Scientists believe Atlantis was destroyed by a **tsunami** thousands of years ago. Tsunamis have been witnessed in this area for centuries.

Plato wrote that Atlantis faced a city named Gadara. This is the ancient name for the city of Cadiz.

According to Plato, the city of Atlantis was an island near the Pillars of Hercules. Today, we know this place as the Straits of Gibraltar. These straits are located off southern Spain.

STOP! THINK...

- After studying these clues, do you think Atlantis has been found?
- What are some ways researchers can learn more about this legendary place?
- Is there any evidence that would convince you that Atlantis existed?

The ruins in this image aren't covered in mud. Could this be how Atlantis looked immediately after the tsunami?

Hundreds of thousands of people visit Angkor Wat every year.

The Temple City

Deep in the jungles of Cambodia lies the city of Angkor Wat. Many know it as Temple City. It is the largest religious monument in the world. It was once home to one million people. But now it is abandoned. The stone temples are covered with moss. The city is in decay. What happened to the people who once lived there? They fled 600 years ago. But why?

Written in the Rings

Researchers analyzed tree rings in the Cambodian jungle. By studying the cores of the trees, they could learn about the climate change that happened centuries ago. The results showed the area around Angkor Wat had suffered severe droughts.

Today, scientists are studying how to best preserve Angkor Watt's beautiful sculptures.

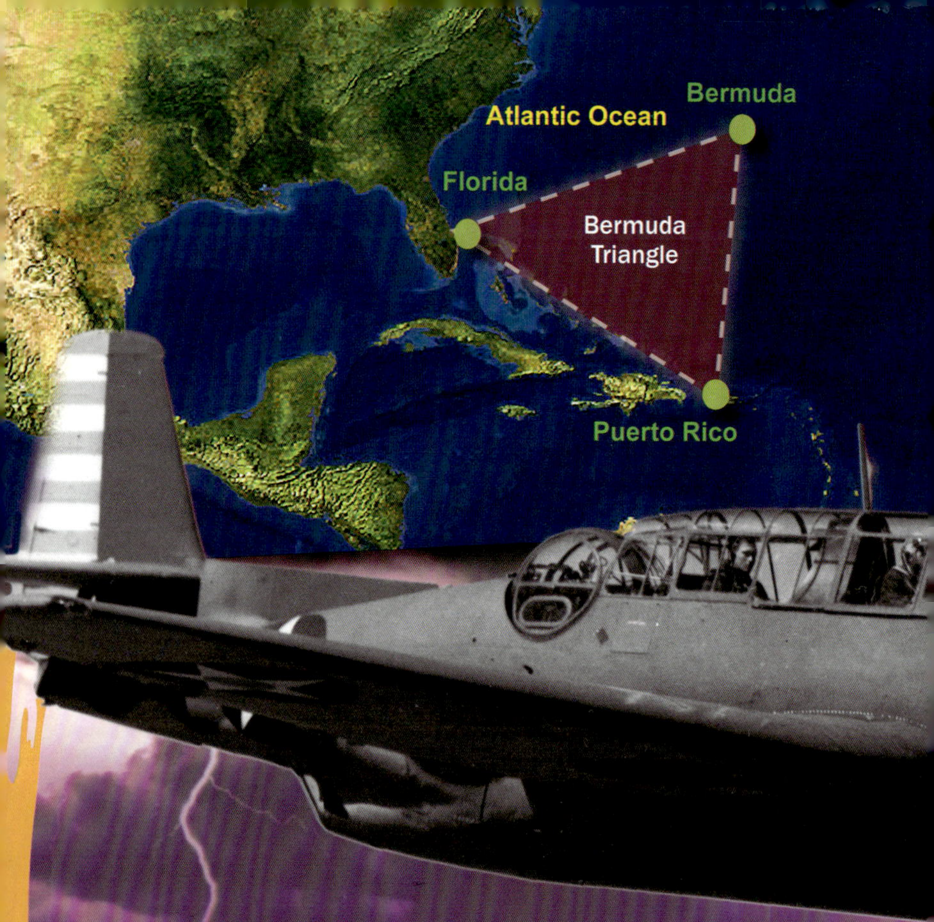

Strange Disappearances

In 1945, five U.S. Navy bombers took off from Florida. They were flying over the Atlantic Ocean. None of them were ever seen again. Since then, dozens of ships and planes have vanished there. This place is known as the Bermuda Triangle. It has given rise to tall tales. Some were stories about sea monsters and giant squid. Some even describe alien **abductions**!

People have suggested many **logical** reasons for the accidents in the Bermuda Triangle. Some blame rough weather. Some blame odd currents. Is there a logical reason for these strange events? Or is something eerie at work?

Another Mysterious Triangle

Off the coast of Japan, many planes and ships have disappeared in the Formosa Triangle. Fishermen call it the Devil's Sea. Compasses behave strangely there, just as they do in the Bermuda Triangle.

Historically Weird

Sailors as far back as Christopher Columbus noted something strange about the Bermuda Triangle region. Columbus wrote in his ship's log about unusual compass bearings there.

Unidentified Visitors

Some of Earth's most puzzling places look pretty normal at first glance. The barren desert of Roswell, New Mexico. A muddy hole in the ground in Canada. But the **mystique** (mi-STEEK) of these sites does not come from large monuments. Nor is it from ancient ruins. These places are interesting because of the people—or beings—who visited them.

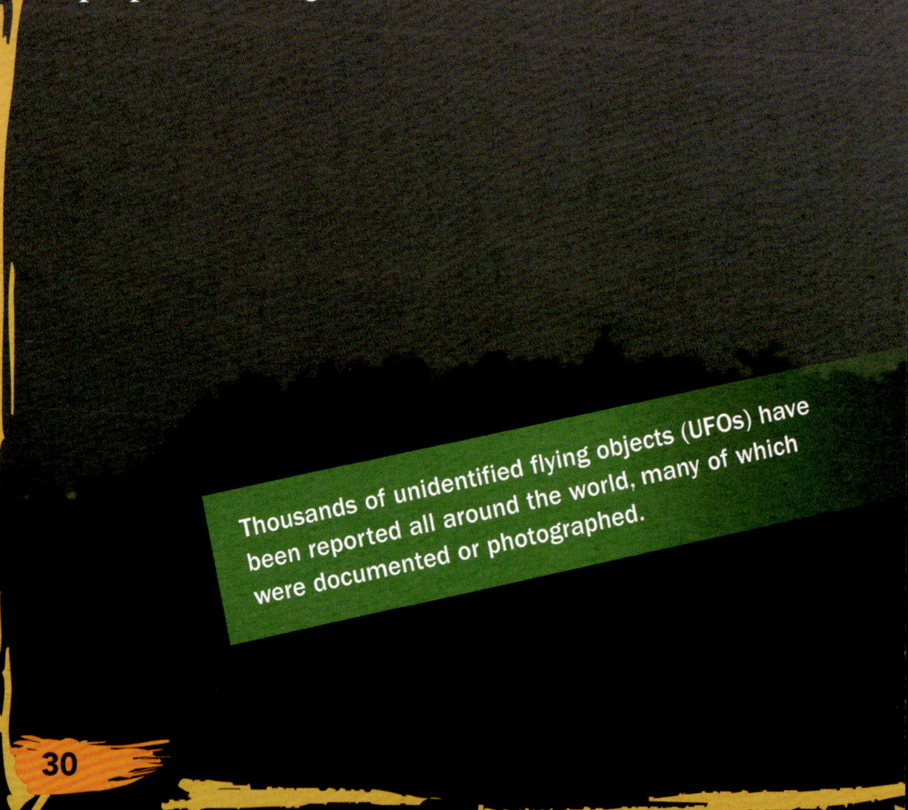

Thousands of unidentified flying objects (UFOs) have been reported all around the world, many of which were documented or photographed.

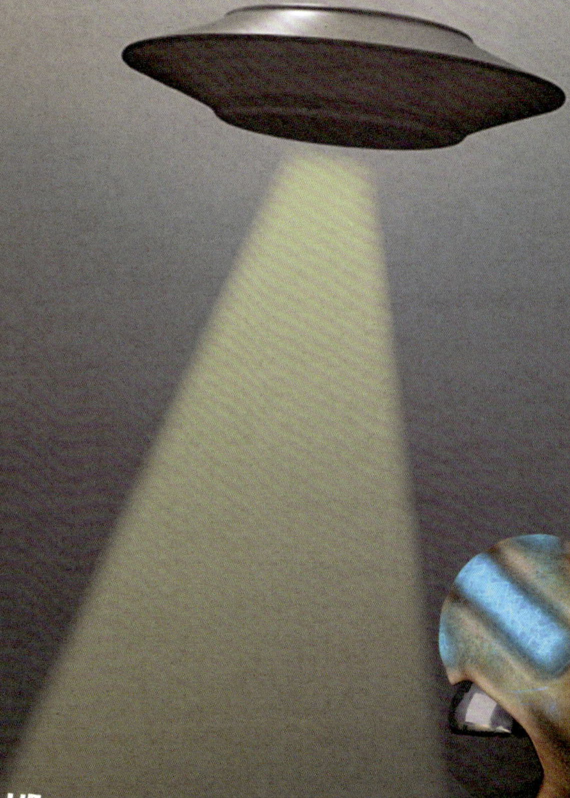

A UFO sighting occurs somewhere on the planet every three minutes.

Prime Minister Winston Churchill reported a strange airship in Kent, England, October 14, 1912. It was the first case of a UFO officially being reported.

Alien Crash Site

In 1947, strange **debris** was found on a ranch near Roswell, New Mexico. People saw shiny silver pieces spread across the desert. The U.S. Army quickly collected them. They sent out an official notice. It said the **wreckage** from a "flying disk" had been found. The next day, the Army withdrew their story and put out a new one. This one said the debris came from a weather balloon.

Many people still believe the first story. They think an alien spaceship crashed in Roswell. Some people even believe aliens were found in the wreck!

Witness Report

In 1950, special agent Guy Hottel wrote a report about flying saucers found in New Mexico.

"They were described as being circular in shape with raised centers, approximately 50 feet in diameter. Each one was occupied by three bodies of human shape but only three feet tall, dressed in a metallic cloth of a very fine texture. Each body was bandaged in a manner very similar to the blackout suits used by speed flyers and test pilots."

The Real X Files

The Federal Bureau of Investigation (FBI) has an online reading room of more than 2,000 files. The files, called *X Files*, used to be **classified**. Now, anyone can read the old reports about investigations into flying discs and the bodies discovered inside them.

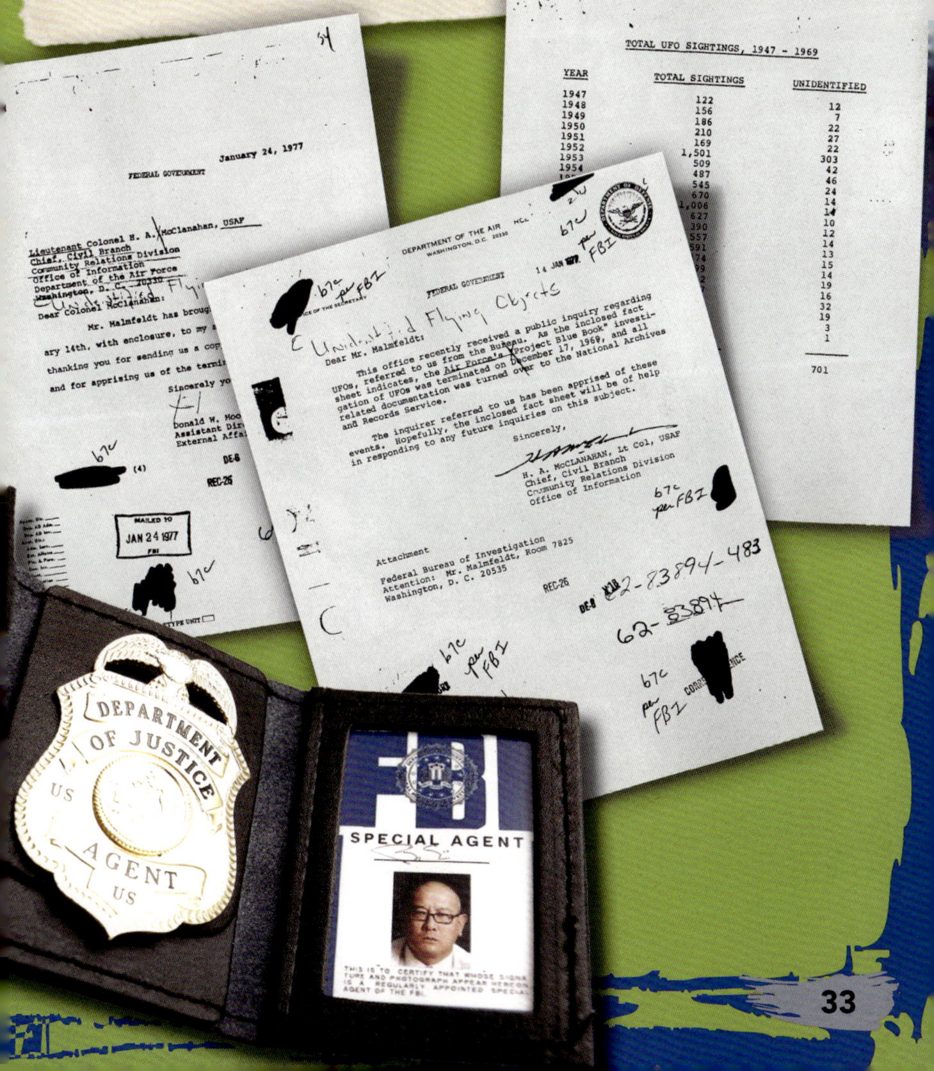

DIG DEEPER!

Looking For Answers

Do these mysterious places spark your curiosity? If you want to try to solve these mysteries, you might consider a career in anthropology, archaeology, astronomy, or Earth sciences.

Astronomers

Astronomers study the universe, including stars and planets. Some astronomers are interested in finding life on other planets. They are called *astrobiologists*.

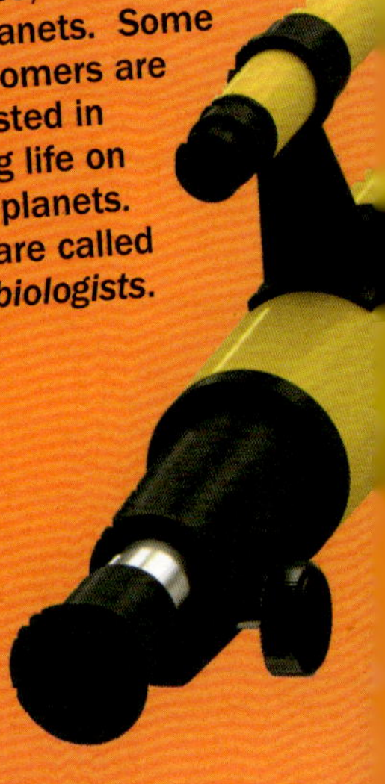

Earth Scientists

Earth scientists study Earth's layers and history. Understanding the Earth has helped us uncover some of the world's strangest mysteries. It can help explain why there are abandoned city ruins. It can also help us understand how a tsunami can sink an entire city.

Archaeologists

Archaeologists study ancient cultures by examining their remains. Howard Carter was the famous archaeologist who discovered the tomb of King Tut in 1922. Inside was the King Tut's mummy and many other treasures that revealed ancient Egyptian life.

Anthropologists

Anthropologists study human culture and history. They answer questions about people who lived long ago by understanding the people who live today. Many anthropologists work in the field and travel to faraway lands. Some cultural anthropologists live with native tribes.

Buried Treasure

In 1795, a teenager found a strange hole on Oak Island, Nova Scotia. The boy had heard stories about pirates in the area. He and some friends went back to the place to dig. They found a layer of stones. Then they found a layer of logs. Had they found buried treasure?

Years later, the young men found a stone tablet in the pit. It was carved with strange symbols. They removed it. And water filled the hole. They tried to dig deeper. But water kept coming in. Many treasure hunters have tried to reach the bottom of the Oak Island Money Pit. But no one has done it.

Treasured Theories

There are many theories about the pit. Some of the most popular theories are that it is:

- the buried treasure of Captain Kidd or Blackbeard
- where the British Army hid money during the American Revolution
- the location of Marie Antoinette's missing jewels.

Captain Kidd on the deck of his ship

Oak Island Money Pit

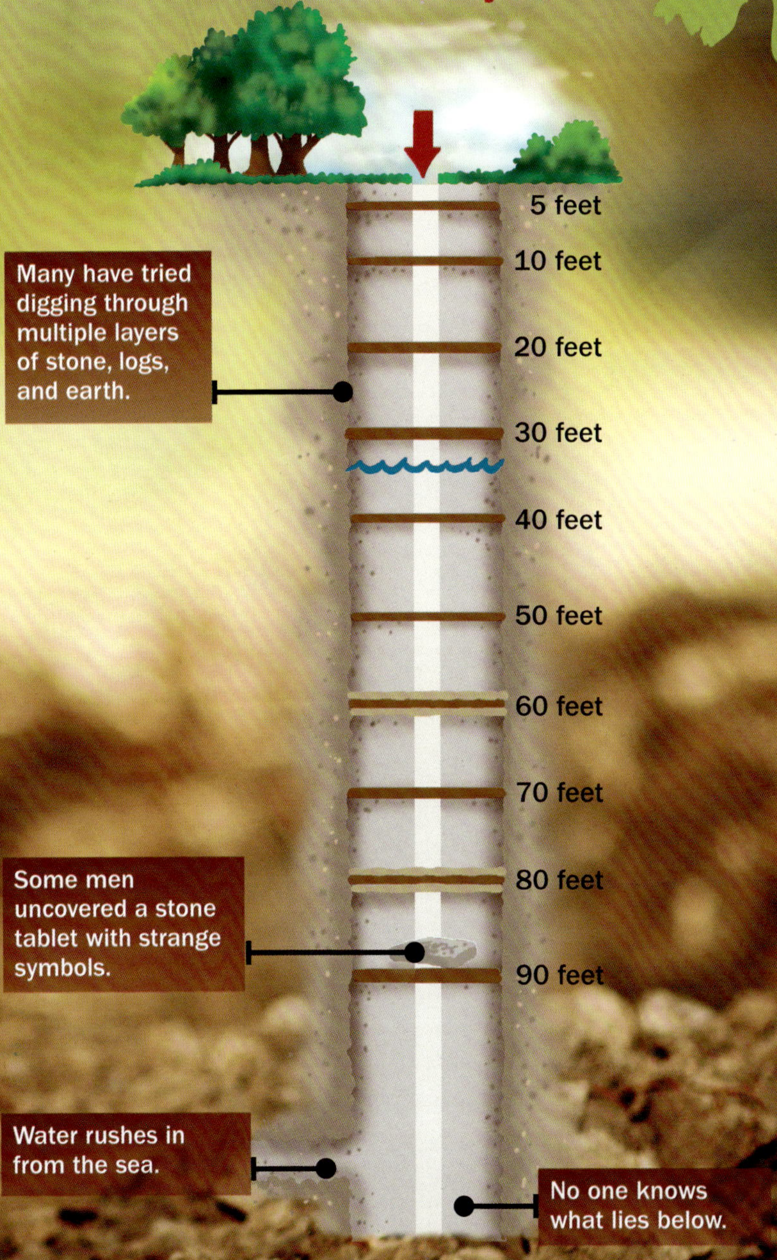

You Solve It!

Investigators use maps to help them explore mysterious places. **Longitude** and **latitude** are an easy way to note the precise location of a place. Longitude is the distance east or west of the **prime meridian** in Greenwich, England. Latitude is the distance at which a place lies north or south of the equator. Both are measured in degrees.

Use these clues to help you identify each mystery. The coordinates will point you in the right direction. Remember to find longitude first and then latitude.

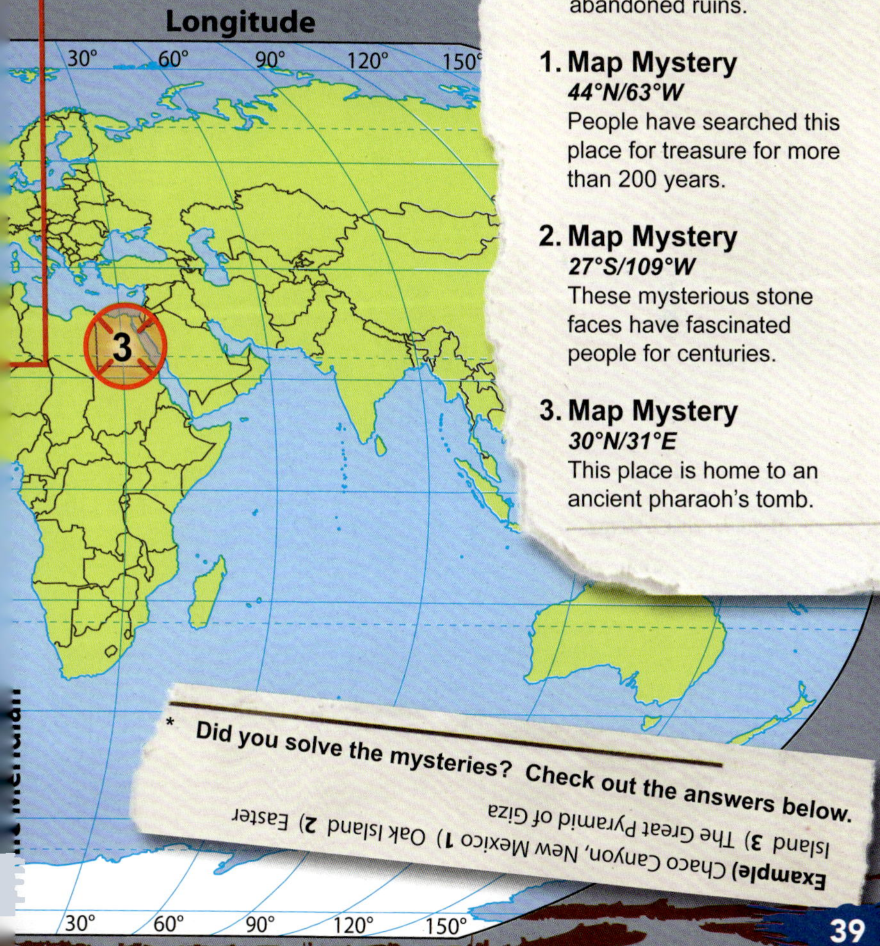

Example
36°N/107°W
This place is home to abandoned ruins.

1. Map Mystery
44°N/63°W
People have searched this place for treasure for more than 200 years.

2. Map Mystery
27°S/109°W
These mysterious stone faces have fascinated people for centuries.

3. Map Mystery
30°N/31°E
This place is home to an ancient pharaoh's tomb.

* **Did you solve the mysteries? Check out the answers below.**

Example) Chaco Canyon, New Mexico **1)** Oak Island **2)** Easter Island **3)** The Great Pyramid of Giza

Unanswered Questions

People have visited nearly every place on Earth. They have gone to the bottom of the ocean. They have walked on the moon. Yet many mysteries remain unsolved. Earth's strangest places fascinate us. Their stories feed our imaginations. And their mysteries inspire us to learn more about our amazing world.

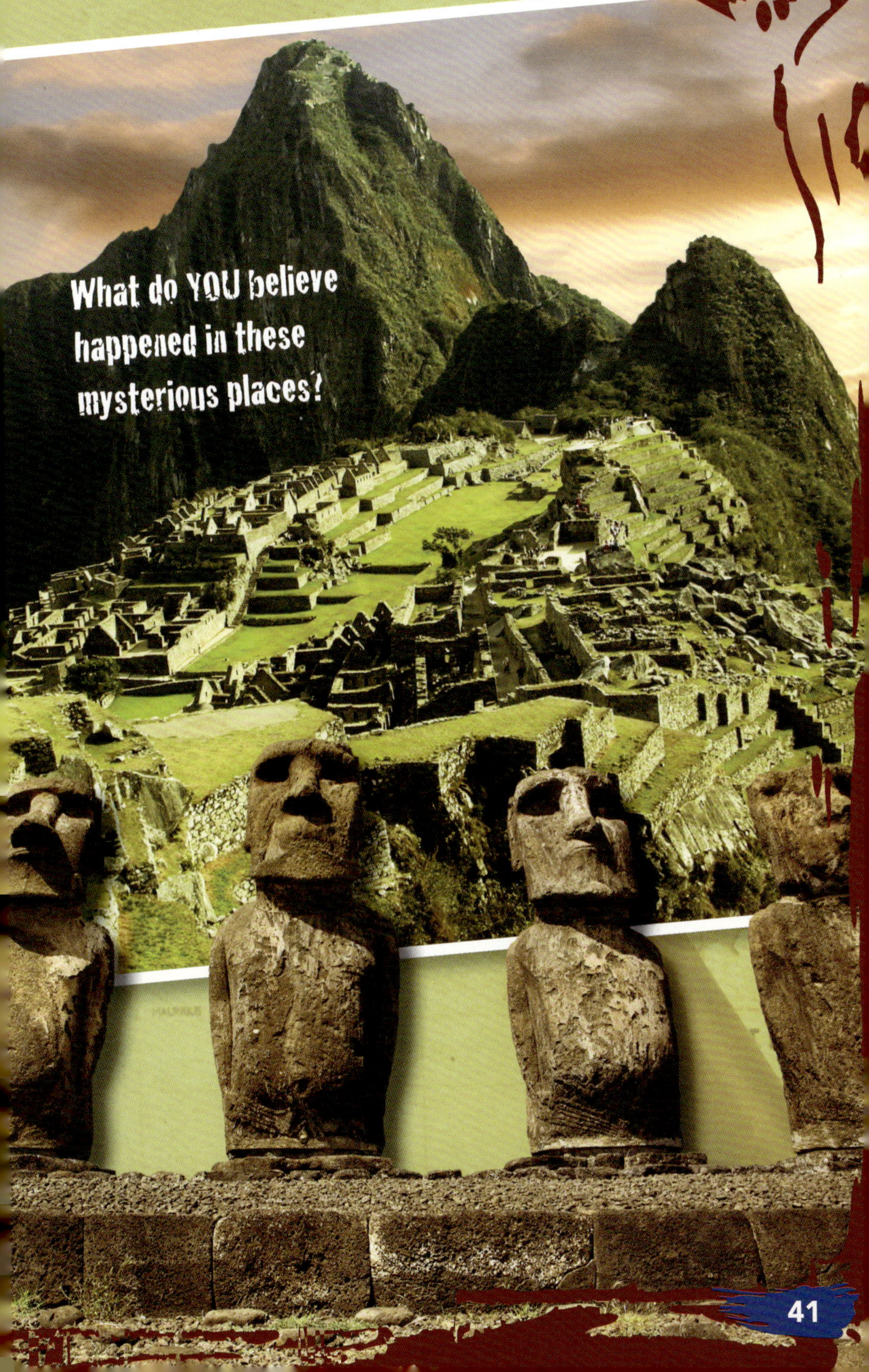
What do YOU believe happened in these mysterious places?

Glossary

abandoned—left behind, usually for safety reasons

abductions—the unlawful carrying away of someone by force or trickery

ancient—very old

archaeologists—scientists who study ancient people and cultures

architects—people who design buildings

astrological—related to the positions of the moon, sun, and planets

chieftains—leaders of groups of people

civilizations—societies that are well-organized

classified—available only to authorized people for reasons of national security

debris—pieces of something that has been broken

drought—a long period of dry weather

hieroglyphics—a system of writing that uses pictures

kivas—underground or partly underground chambers used for ceremonial meetings

latitude—the distance north or south from the Earth's equator, measured in degrees

legendary—having to do with a legend; well-known or famous

logical—sensible or based on facts

longitude—distance measured by degrees east or west from the prime meridian

moai—the name for the large, mysterious stone statues on Easter Island

monuments—things built as tributes to people or events

mystique—a quality that makes something seem mysterious and special

prehistoric—the period of time before events were recorded in writing

prime meridian—the location from which other longitudes are calculated

religious—relating to belief in a higher power

remains—anything that is left over or left behind

solstice—the point in the path of the sun when the sun is farthest north or south

technology—machines and techniques that make work easier for people

tomb—a place for burying a dead person

tsunami—a large destructive ocean wave usually caused by an earthquake

utopia—an ideal place

wreckage—the broken pieces left after something has been damaged

Index

Bibliography

McDaniel, Sean. *Stonehenge*. Bellwether Media, 2012.

Stonehenge has baffled scientists for years. Learn all about this ancient monument and read the theories about how it was created.

Michels, Troy. *Atlantis*. Bellwether Media, 2011.

The lost city of Atlantis was first found in writings from over 2,000 years ago. Since then, there has been much debate about whether the city exists. You can read about the evidence, the debate, and more in this book.

Putnam, James. Geoff Brightling, and Peter Hayman. *Pyramid*. DK Publishing, 2004.

Learn about the mysteries surrounding the pyramids of Giza in Egypt. The photographs in this book help tell the story of these structures and provide clues for how they might have been constructed in the ancient world.

Stewart, Robert. Clint Twist, and Edward Horton. *Mysteries of History*. National Geographic Society, 2003.

This comprehensive look at historical mysteries spans over 5,000 years and includes 19 events or individuals. The Ancient Egyptian Pyramids, the Trojan horse, the Hindenburg explosion, and the Kennedy assassination are all included in this book.

Wencel, Dave. *UFOs*. Bellwether Media, 2010.

This book contains information about UFOs, their sightings, and the debate surrounding them. Learn evidence for and against UFOs to help you make up your mind about these mysterious flying objects!

More to Explore

Kids Gen: Unsolved Mysteries

http://www.kidsgen.com/unsolved_mysteries/

Learn more about historical mysteries on this site. Topics include the Georgia Guidestones, the Bermuda Triangle, and the crystal skulls from the ancient Mayan and Incan ruins.

Ancient Mysteries

http://www.mysteriousplaces.com/

Learn about mysterious ancient ruins, including Stonehenge and Easter Island. Descriptions, photos, and information on all of these ancient sites as well as references to other books are included.

Seven Wonders of the Ancient World

http://kids.nationalgeographic.com/kids/stories/history/ancient-wonders/

Read about the Seven Wonders of the Ancient World on the *National Geographic* website for kids. Colorful photographs and illustrations accompany the descriptions of each location.

Teacher Tube

http://teachertube.com

Teachertube.com is a safe website for teachers to look up videos about whatever you're studying—including mysterious places.

Encyclopedia Britannica for Kids

http://kids.britannica.com/

Encyclopedia Britannica online provides kids with a searchable database of information on any content you are studying in class or would like to know more about. Encyclopedia entries are written for kids ages 8–11 or 11 and up.

About the Authors

Lisa Greathouse grew up in Brooklyn, New York, and graduated from the State University of New York with a bachelor's degree in English and journalism. She was a journalist with The Associated Press for 10 years and covered news on everything from science and technology to business and politics. She has also worked as a magazine editor for the food industry, a website editor for a university, and as the author of many education publications. She is married with two children and resides in Southern California. If she could solve any mystery, she would love to know more about Atlantis

Stephanie Kuligowski has a bachelor's degree in journalism from the University of Missouri and a master's degree in teaching from National Louis University. She worked as a newspaper reporter and columnist before becoming a teacher. Stephanie taught fifth grade for seven years. She lives in Crystal Lake, Illinois, with her husband and their two children. On weekends, she searches for buried treasure.